Drew Weymouth

The Loudness War: A Game and Market Theory Analysis

GRIN Verlag

Bibliografische Information der Deutschen Nationalbibliothek:

Die Deutsche Bibliothek verzeichnet diese Publikation in der Deutschen National-
bibliografie; detaillierte bibliografische Daten sind im Internet über http://dnb.d-
nb.de/ abrufbar.

Imprint:

Copyright © 2012 GRIN Verlag GmbH
Druck und Bindung: Books on Demand GmbH, Norderstedt Germany
ISBN: 978-3-656-34740-8

This book at GRIN:

http://www.grin.com/en/e-book/206816/the-loudness-war-a-game-and-market-
theory-analysis

The Loudness War: A Game and Market Theory Analysis

Drew Weymouth

November 30, 2012

Introduction and History

The "loudness war" is the phenomenon in which loudness levels on commercially-released music recordings have been increasing over time. This is driven by the belief that, all else being equal, the louder of two recordings will be noticed more and preferred by a listener. The loudness war began as early as the 1950s and '60s with 7" 45rpm singles. Jukeboxes playing these singles, which were commonly found in bars and other public places, often had only one preset volume level. Record companies tried to make their singles louder, or "hotter" than their competitors so they would stand out among the others [4].

The practice of making loud masters continued throughout the vinyl era, but it wasn't until the Compact Disc became the dominant format that the loudness war really gained momentum. Unlike an analog recording, with digital audio, there is an absolute limit to the amplitude of a recorded sound wave, above which the wave is sharply truncated or "clipped." This level is designated as 0 dBFS (decibels full-scale), and digital loudness levels are measured in negative dBFS (decibels below full-scale). When referring to dBFS figures, a distinction must be made between *peak level*, which is the level of the loudest points in a recording, and *average* or *RMS level*, which is the average loudness over the entire recording. In the 1980s, the early years of the CD, there was little incentive to create loud masters, but as CDs became more popular,

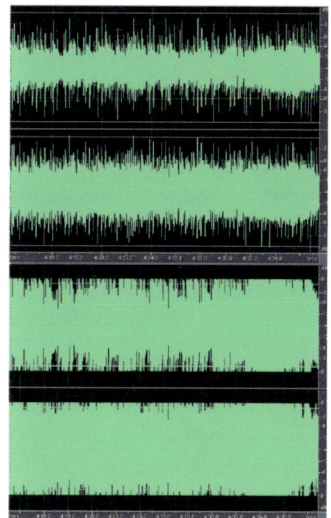

Figure 1: A comparison between loudness levels from two versions of the Red Hot Chili Peppers' song "Give It Away." The top version is from the original 1991 album and the bottom from the 2003 "Greatest Hits" collection. [3]

recording engineers began using digital tools to push the loudness levels higher. For example, in

1987, a CD with an average level of -15 dBFS was considered loud. By 1994, the average level was roughly -12 dBFS, and in 2005 it reached -9 dBFS [8]. In human terms, the average CD in 1987 sounds about half as loud as its 2005 counterpart when played with the same volume setting.

Recording engineers cannot increase loudness levels indefinitely without compromising sound quality. In the 1990s, most recordings already had peak levels that reach 0 dBFS and cannot be made louder. In order to continue increasing average loudness, engineers resort to two tools: *peak limiting* and *dynamic range compression*. Peak limiting is the process of reducing the level of individual peaks in a recording, while dynamic range compression reduces the difference between loud sections and quiet sections in a recording, so that the recording as a whole sounds louder. Both of these techniques have negative effects on the audio fidelity. Peak limiting reshapes the loudest peaks, destroying the musical transients they represent, while dynamic range compression drastically reduces the contrast between loud and soft sections in a recording. Musicians and listeners alike have criticized these practices of "hyper-compression." For example, musician Bob Dylan has stated: "You listen to these modern records, they're atrocious, they have sound all over them. There's no definition of nothing, no vocal, no nothing, just like—static" [4]. But the loudness war continues on, and CD volume levels continue to increase.

Why the Loudness War?

One may ask why the record companies partake in the loudness war given the negative impact it has on sound quality. Isn't recorded music supposed to be as clear and true to a live performance as possible? Simply put, the reason for the loudness war is that record companies believe that loud music sells better. In fact, there is evidence that in some cases listeners do associate loudness with quality [1]. There are several examples of commercially successful loud albums. The widely popular 1995 album by Oasis, *(What's the Story) Morning Glory?*, had tracks reaching -8 dBFS RMS, which at the time was an astonishing level [4]. Today, many people listen to music primarily in the car or other noisy places, where louder music cuts through against the background noise. Record companies, especially today, tend to cater to this market of casual, "on-the-go" listeners and make heavy use of compression and limiting in order to make their album louder.

Let's consider the loudness war as a two-player strategic game. The players are two different record companies, each producing a CD. Each record company has two strategies: release a loud CD (L) and release a quiet CD (Q). We can construct the following symmetric payoff matrix for this scenario.

CD 2

		L	Q
CD 1	L	(a, a)	(b, c)
	Q	(c, b)	(d, d)

2

The values of a, b, c, and d for this game must satisfy the constraint $b > d > a > c$. This is because, under the belief that a louder album will sell more than a quieter album, a record company receives the maximum payoff when they produce a loud CD and their competitor releases a quiet CD. Conversely, the company releasing the quiet CD receives the minimum payoff because they are outsold by their competitor. If both release a loud album, we will assume that they will split sales evenly and receive the same payoff. If both produce a quiet CD, they still sell evenly, but their payoff is slightly higher because their CDs sound better than they would have had they been subjected to limiting and compression. Upon analysis of this payoff matrix, we see that no matter what the actual values of a–d are, (L, L) is the only *Nash equilibrium* in the game. This means that the case in which both companies release a loud CD is the only case in which neither can improve their payoff singlehandedly by switching their strategy. This result is an archetypal example of the famous *Prisoner's dilemma* — a theoretical two-player strategic game in which the two players may not cooperate, even if it seems to be in their best interest [6]. For the loudness war game, Q can be thought of as the "cooperate" strategy and L the "defect" strategy. Even though (Q, Q) is better for both players than (L, L), they will, with high probability, both play L.

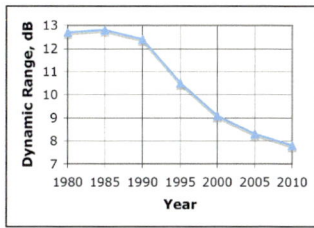

Figure 2: A plot showing the decline of dynamic range in commercial recordings over time as a result of the continued escalation of the loudness war. [9]

Further analysis of this payoff matrix reveals that in addition, L is an *evolutionarily stable* strategy — a strategy (call it S) with the property that if the majority of the population is playing S, no small group of "foreign invaders" playing a different strategy can thrive. The converse also holds: if the majority of the population is playing some strategy T, and S is an evolutionarily stable strategy, a small group of invaders playing S will thrive and eventually overtake those playing T. For the symmetric payoff matrix above, the condition for L to be an evolutionarily stable strategy is that either (i) $a > c$ or (ii) $a = c$ and $b > d$ [2]. Since criterion (i) holds for the loudness war game, releasing a loud CD is evolutionarily stable. This explains why, despite the drawbacks with respect to sound quality, the vast majority of record companies and mastering engineers today choose to utilize heavy peak limiting and dynamic range compression to make loud albums.

The CD Market: A Market for Lemons

We now consider the loudness war and its effect on consumers — those who purchase and listen to music. The majority of these consumers are casual listeners, who play music as background while doing other tasks, or in noisy environments such as a car, bus, or subway. Most of these listeners are not directly affected by the loudness war. They do not hear the difference between hyper-compressed and quieter, dynamic music, and many are not even aware of the loudness war's existence. However, there are also two additional groups of listeners: those who do hear and dislike the effects of hyper-compression, and those who are gradually becoming aware of the loudness war and its negative impact on audio fidelity [5]. In 2008, the heavy metal band Metallica released *Death Magnetic*, an album which drew severe criticism for its excessive distortion and hyper-compression. Over 22,000 music fans signed an online petition requesting that the album be remastered and re-released at a lower volume level [5]. Audio engineer Earl Vickers has researched and analyzed the loudness war extensively, and at the 129th Audio Engineering Society Convention, he presented a paper in which he concludes that, despite the dominant belief held by record companies, loudness is *not* positively correlated with sales, and in fact the opposite may be true as some listeners do prefer more dynamic music [9]. Let's analyze the market for CDs and examine why this is the case.

For the majority of listeners who are not aware of, or are ambivalent to, the effects of the loudness war, their participation in the music market is unchanged. But for active listeners and audiophiles, the value they place on a CD purchase is diminished by the loudness war. When purchasing an album, such a consumer will not know whether that album is properly mastered or is a casualty of the loudness war, with compressed and distorted sound. What results is a scenario similar to the used car "market for lemons" discussed in Easley and Kleinberg's *Networks, Crowds, and Markets.* These consumers must consider that with every purchase, there is some probability p that they purchase a well-mastered CD, and probability $1 - p$ that they purchase a "lemon." Consumers will have some value G that they place on good CDs. They will purchase a good CD if its price is at or below this value. Similarly, they have some value B that they place on bad CDs. Since good CDs and bad CDs are indistinguishable at the time of purchase, consumers will value all CDs equally with value V, where

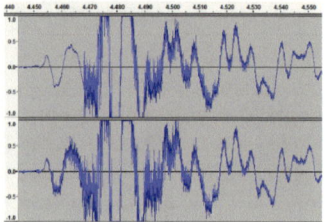

Figure 3: A severely clipped drum beat from Michael Jackson's "Billie Jean," remastered in 2008.

$$V = p \cdot G + (1 - p) \cdot B$$

We have already seen that, for record companies, producing loud (bad) CDs is the dominant strategy. So the probability p of purchasing a good CD is being driven towards zero. Consequently, the value V that a critical listener places on a CD is driven towards B, their value for bad CDs. It is easy to see that the market equilibrium is (theoretically) one in which only bad CDs are sold.

The casual listeners who are not affected by the loudness war do not make a distinction between good CDs and bad CDs. To them, all CDs are "good," so, despite a market filled with loud CDs, these listeners still have the same value for a CD as they would if all the CDs were not loud.

4

Therefore, the record companies and music stores have very little incentive to lower their sales price below the critical listeners' value since the casual listeners are still driving the market. So the loudness war can result in an overall decline in album sales. Music fans who care about dynamic, natural sounding music have been driven out of the market. Their value for CDs has dropped, but market prices have not dropped because the majority of consumers have not changed their purchasing behavior.

Figure 4: The Turn Me Up! certification logo. [10]

In their discussion of the "market for lemons," Easley and Kleinberg show that if there is a certification system in place such that purchasers can distinguish the "lemons" from the good items, market balance can be to some extent restored. If a critical listener can be certain that a certain CD is not hyper-compressed, they are willing to pay a higher price for it. Such a certification system does in fact exist for the CD market, though it is still in its infancy. In 2007, Charles Dye, John Ralston, and Allen Wagner founded Turn Me Up! which is a nonprofit organization whose mission is to help make releasing quieter, dynamic albums a commercially viable option. They have created a system in which albums which meet certain criteria for dynamic range can display a Turn Me Up! sticker, informing the purchaser that the album has not been hyper-compressed for the sake of loudness [10]. There are also audiophile record labels, such as Mobile Fidelity Sound Lab (MFSL) which specialize in producing well-mastered high-quality albums for the niche market of critical listeners.

Ending the Loudness War: Changing the Payoffs

The loudness war has been waging on for nearly half a century, but it may finally be drawing to a close. While audiophile record labels and dynamic range certification have allowed quieter albums to coexist with louder ones on the market, they do not directly address the problem of hyper-compressed CDs existing in the first place. The loudness war arose because for record companies, producing loud albums is a dominant strategy. The war can be ended by changing the payoff matrix so that loud is no longer an advantage. The open ReplayGain standard, and Apple's proprietary Sound Check, may be doing just that. Introduced in 2001, ReplayGain is a standard to gauge the perceived loudness of audio tracks, and automatically adjust the volume upon playback so that tracks mastered with different levels are heard at equal loudness [7]. When enabled, both of these standards raise the level of quiet tracks, and lower the level of loud tracks. This effectively neutralizes the advantage that loud mastering has over quiet, but it cannot undo the effects of limiting and compression. Therefore, hyper-compressed albums sound no louder, but still retain the unpleasant distortion and loss of dynamic contrast. SoundCheck is supported in iTunes and all iPod devices. ReplayGain is supported in many digital audio players as well. In addition, online streaming music services such as Spotify offer similar forms of loudness normalization.

With loudness normalization in place, we need to reconsider the symmetric two-player payoff matrix for the loudness war and examine how it has changed. The structure of the game is the same as before:

CD 2

		L	Q
CD 1	L	(a,a)	(b,c)
	Q	(c,b)	(d,d)

However, the constraint on a–d has become $c > d > a > b$ — in essence the reverse of the case without loudness normalization. In this new situation, quieter CDs will be preferred and will sell better, since they do not suffer from distortion and reduced dynamic range, but sound equally loud as loudly mastered CDs. Therefore, the new Nash equilibrium for this game is (Q, Q) and releasing quiet albums is the dominant strategy for a record company. There is no incentive to sacrifice sound quality with compression and limiting if there is no associated loudness gain. If loudness normalization continues to be utilized and eventually becomes commonplace, we should expect to see average volume levels begin to fall, and dynamic range and clarity restored to recorded music. By changing the payoffs in the loudness war game, the volume control will once again be returned to where it belongs: in the hands of the listener.

References

[1] Andry, Tom. "How to Skew a Blind Listening Test." *Audioholics Magazine.* 08 September 2009. Web. <http://www.audioholics.com/buying-guides/how-to-shop/how-to-skew-a-blind-listening-test>

[2] Easley, David and Jon Kleinberg. *Networks, Crowds, and Markets.* New York: Cambridge University Press, 2010. Print.

[3] "'Give It Away' Loudness Comparison." Image from *Wikimedia Commons.* 19 May 2010. Web. <http://commons.wikimedia.org/wiki/File:GiveItAwayLoudnessComparison.png>

[4] "Loudness War." *Wikipedia, The Free Encyclopedia.* Wikimedia Foundation, Inc. 12 November 2012. Web. <http://en.wikipedia.org/wiki/Loudness_war>

[5] "The Loudness War — An Open Letter to the Music Industry." *Turn Me Up!* Web. <http://www.turnmeup.org>

[6] "Prisoner's dilemma." *Wikipedia, The Free Encyclopedia.* Wikimedia Foundation, Inc. 28 November 2012. Web. <http://en.wikipedia.org/wiki/Prisoner's_dilemma>

[7] "ReplayGain." *Wikipedia, The Free Encyclopedia.* Wikimedia Foundation, Inc. 25 November 2012. Web. <http://en.wikipedia.org/wiki/ReplayGain>

[8] Southall, Nick. "Imperfect Sound Forever." *Stylus Magazine.* 01 May 2006. Web. <http://www.stylusmagazine.com/articles/weekly_article/imperfect-sound-forever.htm>

[9] Vickers, Earl. "The Loudness War: Background, Speculation and Recommendations." *129th Audio Engineering Society Convention.* 4 November 2010. Web. <http://www.sfxmachine.com/docs/loudnesswar/>

[10] "Who We Are." *Turn Me Up!* Web. <http://www.turnmeup.org/about_us.shtml>